BEYOND OUR TIME

What The Bible Says About America In Prophecy

NORMAN W. MATHERS

Copyright 1998 by Norman W. Mathers

All rights reserved. Published by ATS Publications.

Reproduction or translation of any part of this work beyond that permitted by Section 107 or 108 of the United States Copyright Act without the permission of the copyright owner is unlawful. Requests for permission or further information should be addressed to the Permissions Department, ATS Publications, 62 Chase Circle, Willow Springs, NC 27592.

This publication is designed to provide accurate and authoritative information in regard to the subject matter covered. It is sold with the understanding that the publisher is not engaged in rendering legal, accounting, or other professional service. If legal advice or other assistance is required, the services of a competent professional person should be sought. From a Declaration of Principles jointly adapted by a Committee of the American Bar Association and a Committee of Publishers.

Library of Congress Catalog Card Number 98-093747

Mathers, Norman W.,
 -    by Norman W. Mathers.
p. cm.
ISBN 0-9634654-2-2 (paper) :
1. Bible Prophecies - America. 2. The United States in Bible Prophecy.
I. Title.

Manufactured in the United States of America
AGF-PA
987654321

TABLE OF CONTENTS

1. IS AMERICA IN PROPHECY? 1
2. AMERICA IS IN PROPHECY 9
3. THE BALANCE OF POWER 20
4. SILENCE 30
5. WILL AMERICA BE DESTROYED BY A NUCLEAR ATTACK? 37
6. WHY DOES AMERICA REMAIN? 42
7. IT'S FIXED! 46
8. THE TIMES AND THE SEASONS 50
9. AMERICA IN THE POST CHRISTIAN ERA 57
10. AMERICA AT PRESENT - THE DEFENSE QUESTION 63
11. AMERICA'S SEAL JUDGEMENTS 69
12. AMERICA IN THE MIDDLE EAST 76
13. MYSTERY BABYLON THE GREAT 81
14. AMERICA EXISTS 97
15. GOD AND AMERICA 103
16. AMERICA'S GRAVE DANGER 112

1

IS AMERICA IN PROPHECY?

Some Bible expositors have answered this question in the negative. No, America is not mentioned in Bible prophecy. Others have affirmed that America is found in the prophecies of the Bible based on general evidence. This present book, *Beyond Our Time, America In Prophecy* is a fresh examination of biblical evidence and other supporting research.

Don't Bother Me With The Facts, My Mind Is Made Up!

Those who say that America is not in the Bible are the "chapter and verse people." By this, I mean that they would ask for a chapter and verse on this subject. Although "chapter-and-verse-people" are not wrong, their true need, as is ours, is to be able to answer the question "Is America in Prophecy?" with reasoning from the scriptures. The best biblical example of reasoning from the scriptures was the apostle, Paul. Would Paul do less? We read in the Bible that Paul reasoned that Jesus was the Christ and proved that he was the long awaited Messiah.

Scholarship Can Develop This Question

Even the admission of America in bible prophecy based on general evidence has to be developed to fully come to established conclusions on the subject. Some admit that America is in prophecy based on general scriptural evidence.*
* J. F. Walvoord, *The Nations In Prophecy*, p. 172.
However, the thing to do is to shy away from this question because there may be other more important prophecies. America in prophecy, in general thinking in some circles may be considered to sensational.

Beyond Our Time, America in Prophecy reasons within the boundaries of the end-time prophecies. Bible expositors, often lacking rational skills and training in scholarship, have shied away from the question. Intuition tells me as I begin to write this work that America has been declining as these end time world events are coming about. This, of course, is only intuition without sufficient evidence to test the intuition.

America in Prophecy

Our beloved country is very dear to us, so the need to develop this question as to America in prophecy has never been greater. The Bible tells us to pray for our country, our president and our rulers; to pay our taxes, to be in submission to these divine servants, and to live in civil obedience to the laws of the land.

Enough biblical evidence is available - if reasoned through based on the perimeters and area of bible prophecies - to come to conclusions that are very definite in nature.

The Bible On America In Prophecy Ignored

This question as to America in prophecy has been ignored because of the principle of conformity. The general consensus is either chapter and verse please, or it is very general in nature. The answer is there if reasoned within the perimeters, the boundaries, and the area set forth in the Bible. Prophets, such as John in The Revelation, Ezekiel, and Zechariah, have spoken definitely about America in Prophecy.

Radio Talk Shows And Interviews

This question of America in prophecy has been asked repeatedly on radio talk shows and interviews. Even back from August to December of 1993, this question arose in more than twenty talk shows and interviews across the country.

Hot Topic

While prophecy is a hot topic at present, the question of whether America is in prophecy is a question of even greater interest to a vast majority of people. This is good because after all America is a wonderful country and we are all concerned about the future of our country and our own future.

Bible Scholarship And Rationalism

A very definite answer can be arrived at as to American in prophecy. Revelation chapter 12 speaks very definitely of America in prophecy. This principle is being demonstrated and verified at the present time in our current history. Yet bible expositors, often untrained in rationalism, have not reasoned their way through the material that needs to be reflected upon.

Kant On Rationalism

Immanuel Kant, the philosopher, argued that the justification for what men do must be a worthy reason. Reason that is subjected to revelation provides clear answers to the treatment of any material. By a scholarly treatment of the material, the question being reflected upon can be reasoned through.

Biblically Based

Reason, rationalism, and reflection upon the Bible is necessary. While reason must always be the servant of revelation, yet so often reason and rationalism are discarded as unnecessary and unworthy of our time and consideration. Did Paul the Apostle reason with men from the scriptures? He did! The Canon closed about 90 A.D. in the first century. No further revelation has been given since that time. However, reason is often a helpful tool to arrive at sought after answers.

America In Ezekiel 38:13

Bible expositors have avoided Ezekiel's clear reference to America. In the same context, a very definite list is given as to the northern confederacy, a Russian - African - Arab power block.

Sufficient material from varied disciplines supported by the doctrine of reason based on scripture will bring us to a very definite conclusion.

Russia Attacks Israel

Russia is identified clearly in Ezekiel based on the grammar of the text as the nation that comes from the farthest point out of the north. Even if one rejects the grammatical basis for certain identification of Russia, Gog will come from the remotest parts of the north down into the land of Israel. The nation that is the farthest point due north from Israel today is Russia.

America Is In Ezekiel 38

Ezekiel points to the nations that give only a verbal rebuke a political rebuke against the invasion of Israel.

A Sudden Change In Plans

The Hebrew prophet predicts that the Russian change in policy is a sudden one that marks a distinct turn in their previous political plans.*

This Russian invasion of Israel is for the purpose of gaining plunder, spoils, and booty. Given the modern economic plight of Russia, such is not hard to believe.*

The merchants of Tarshish and the young lions, Sheba and Dedan have been interpreted as nations that have come and gone on the world stage. This interpretation is faulty because Ezekiel is speaking of an event that is yet future even to our day. It makes no sense whatsoever to apply these nations to old biblical nations that are no longer in existence today.

* Ezekiel 38:10; 38:12.

The Russian invasion of Israel is yet future and generally agreed by scholars to occur at the midpoint of the tribulation. The tribulation, lasting seven years, begins when the western world dictator and the world church make a peace accord with Israel. The reader may want to read *Beyond Desert Storm* for an understanding of the divine framework in which these end time events occur.

Political Consensus

A consensus is given by Sheba, Dedan, the merchants of Tarshish, and the young lions justifying the Russian invasion of Israel as a worthy purpose because they have sufficient rationale for this military invasion. Russian military aggression is nothing new even in our day. Russian invasion of Afghanistan and also Ethiopia is historical fact. Failure to understand the revolutionary principles of unprovoked aggression and continued propaganda is to not understand some very basic Russian Marxist Lenin doctrines.

The Young Lions

America fits the category of all the young lions. Ezekiel's words strike the very origins of America as originating with great Britain and prior to the American revolution as a member of the commonwealth. All members of the British commonwealth along with America wield only a political rhetoric against this Russian-European-African-Arab power block coming against poor defenseless Israel.

Even if a definite conclusion could not be arrived at after the material has been reasoned through, fewer possibilities would remain as to America in prophecy.

Such well-known Theologians as Dr. John F. Walvoord in his book *The Nations in Prophecy* point out the sufficiency of evidence in the Bible to conclude the role of America in end time world events.*

The Question Can Be Answered

The question before us as to whether America is in prophecy can be answered based on modern scholarship, reasoning through the many varied avenues of supporting biblical evidence and other helpful disciplines. The strongest biblical arguments will become self-evident.

In the next exciting chapter, the Bible speaks to the subject of America in prophecy.

STUDY QUESTIONS

1. What is the major purpose of the book *Beyond Our Time?*
2. Why do some people think America is not in bible prophecy?
3. What approach does the author take to prove America is in prophecy?
4. What two factors help us to arrive at the definite conclusion America is in prophecy?
5. What does Ezekiel 38:13 tell us about America in Prophecy?
6. What nation is the farthest point due north from Israel?
7. What response does America give to the Russian invasion?
8. Who are the young lions of Ezekiel 38?
9. What conclusion does the author reach about America at the end of chapter 1?

2

AMERICA IS IN PROPHECY

America is very definitely found in prophecy in Ezekiel: Sheba, Dedan, the merchants of Tarshish and the young lions. the context of Ezekiel 38 & 39 is a prophecy against Russia, the king of the north and her satellites. The nations mentioned in Ezekiel 38 can be easily identified as modern nations that are with us today. All the Old Testament prophets set their face against Russia and her allies as they would play their role in end time elect events.* The Hebrew word Rosh has within it the consonants of Russia, the work Meschech traced through vowel changes comes to Moschoi and Moscow. Tubal has long been identified as a modern province in Russia. America, while not a Russian ally, is found in this context of powers in the end times.

Put is the modern day Libya. Lud is representative of African nations. Cush is known to be present day Ethiopia. All Arabia, an ally of Egypt, will support Russia and the Russian invasion of Israel. Persia is Iran, a Russian ally during the events of the end times. The Bible speaks of one Germany, not two in this end time political scenario. The Talmud identifies Gomer as Germany. Beth-togarmah is modern day Turkey, a Russian ally long known to be communist.*

*Ezekiel 38

Faulty Hermeneutics

Bible expositors of the past have not dealt with the identification of Sheba, Dedan, the merchants of Tarshish and all the young lions in terms of modern day. They have relegated it to a meaning in the historical past. This doesn't make sense because the context is a future context, even future to our day.

Saudi Arabia, And The ECC

The kingdom of Sheba and Dedan would be best understood as Saudi Arabia. The merchants of Tarshish may well be the modern day United States of Europe the final form of the economic common market. The earlier form of the merchants of Tarshish would be the Old British Colonies. Although generally Tarshish is best identified as Spain or Europe.* Only the voice of the young lions is heard in the face of this Russian military invasion of Israel.

Tarshish

The Phoenician work comes from the Akkadian having to do with smelting plants and refineries. Ships, trade and merchants are also an acceptable nuance of the word. Given the Old Testament background of Solomon, these ocean freighters were involved in the hauling of precious metals and materials from European, Mediterranean or Middle Eastern ports.*

*M. F. Unger, Unger's Bible Dictionary, pp. 258. 1006. 1070

America, One Of The Young Lions, Continues As A Nation

America is spoken of here as one of the young lions. Retrogression and a recessed condition of the nation is spoken of rather than the lion which was to be the kingpin of the nations. Nevertheless, America continues in existence as a nation, although in a weakened condition, during the tribulation period.

More On Tarshish

In 2 Chronicles 9:21, the ships of Tarshish brought treasures not from Spain but Africa. Such treasures were sold in the Middle East. Tarshish is translated Karkedonos in the Greek Septuagint which was the Greek paradigm of Carthage in North Africa.

Tarshish settled in Spain establishing a trading port there for a stopover point on their way to the Eastern Mediterranean.*

A Grandson Of Japheth

Tarshish was a grandson of Japheth who was one of Noah's three sons. Japheth's descendants are Indo-European. Keilisch is correct when he says that Tarshish is a name used as a figure of speech to stand for all of Europe. Javan is used to designate all the Greeks. Tarshish is not to be understood as the Phoenicians. The Phoenicians were not descendants of Japheth. According to the Greek historian Herodotus, the trading port of

Tarshish was already in existence when these traders known as Phoenicians came there.

Tarshish Is Great Britain

While the emblem of Great Britain has been known to be the lion, the young lions refer to those colonies and members of the commonwealth that have their roots with Great Britain. The understanding of the young lions as all the colonies of Europe is too wide an interpretation. America's roots can be traced not only in terms of origin to Great Britain but also to many citizens who are descendants of the British Isles.

America In Prophecy

The important point is that while these nations and traders recognize the purpose of the invasion of this Russian power block, they are powerless to stop it. A political rhetoric is wielded against this invasion as is similar already to American policy against moves made even in our day by Russia and China.

Three Great Signs Appear In The Heavens

Three signs appear in the heavens that further picture America for us during the end times.

The first sign in the Apocalypse is that of a woman. This woman is wearing the sun. The moon is under the woman's feet. She wears a crown with twelve stars. The woman is with a male child who is ready to be born.

*Arthur C. Custance, Noah's Three Sons, pp. 81-100.

Another Sign In Heaven

A great red dragon who has seven heads and ten horns. The seven heads of the dragon had seven diadems. These crowns signify royalty.

One Third Of The Stars

The red dragon drew one third of the stars of the heavens with his tail. He throws these stars to the Earth. The dragon is waiting to kill the woman's child as soon as he is born.

Before the dragon can kill the male child he is snatched away being caught up to God and his throne.

What Happens To The Woman?

She flees into the wilderness where the Lord God prepared for her a place. The woman will be cared for, for a period of 1,260 days or three and a half years.

A Third Sign

Michael, the archangel and his angels waged war with the dragon and his angels. Michael and his angels win. The dragon and his angels are cast out of heaven. This chapter in Revelation carries with it a number of figures of speech that must be interpreted within the context.

Where Does America Come In?

The woman is given the two wings of the great eagle to get her into the wilderness. God has not only foreordained this event but also the means to accomplishing the event.

The great red dragon is also called the serpent. The serpent's purpose is to drown the woman. The earth opened its mouth to swallow the flood. The great dragon went forth with vengeance to do battle against the woman and her seed. The dragon stood upon the sand of the sea.

A Beast Comes Up

A beast comes up from the sea having ten horns and seven heads. What an ugly creature this beast is!

The Allegory Explained

This apocalyptic book, Revelation, can be understood because it is a revelation. The literal, normal, plain meaning of the chapter is to be taken at face value. If parts of the chapter cannot be understood literally then it should be understood as a figure of speech. The purpose of a figure of speech is to convey a literal message that can be rationally understood.

The Woman is Israel

Anyone familiar with the Old Testament will realize the woman is Israel. The symbology here in Revelation, chapter 12 is used from Joseph's dream.

The Great Red Dragon

The great red dragon is Satan. The red dragon is identified as such later on in Revelation, chapter 20. The dragon wanted to kill the woman's male child being Jesus Christ.

The male child was snatched away before Satan could do so, and he persecutes the woman instead. This persecution of the Jew is under the figure of speech of the flood. The woman fled to a divine place of safety prepared for her from before the world began. The earth, the Gentiles, and the nations, helped the Jews in this time of further anti-semitic persecution.

The Dragon's Wrath

The wrath of the dragon was so fierce against the male child, Jesus Christ, because He is to rule on the earth for a period of 1000 years.

Michael The Archangel

He is appointed as protector over the people of Israel. Satan is cast out of heaven losing his battle against Michael and his angels. This great dragon is also called the old serpent, the devil, and Satan. Michael the good archangel goes to war with Satan and his demons.

Satan The Great Deceiver

Satan is the one who deceives the whole world. The Greek word here is oikoumene which is the world of men and women. The word ecumenical is an English derivative of this Greek word.

The Heavens Rejoice

The heavens rejoice, but this casting out of Satan out of heaven is a definite divine judgement to the earth and the sea. The wrath of the devil is directed against the earth with great intensity. The great red dragon knows his time is short.

The Two Wings Of The Great Eagle

This aid is given to the woman who is Israel to help her escape the fierce dragon. The two wings of the great eagle is America.

This figure of speech is a direct reference to America. America befriends the Jews in this the worst anti-semitic purge of all times! America persuades the other nations to befriend the Jew. The combined effort of the nations of the earth swallows up the serpent's flood. America is able to rescue Israel from this terrible time of suffering and persecution.

A Monster Emerges

The great red dragon goes forth with special wrath against the seed of the woman. The dragon stands on the sand of the sea. Suddenly up out of the sea, a monster emerges. Water sprays everywhere! This ugly brute has ten horns, and seven heads. Upon his heads are ten diadems, crowns that signify royalty. The great red dragon gives up his authority, rule and power to the beast.

Why Are The Two Wings Of The Eagle America?

The two wings of the eagle is America because the context of the apocalypse is dealing with nations.

The woman is Israel. The earth is the nations of the world. The great red eagle in Ezekiel 17 is the nation Babylon. Revelation 12 is not fulfilled but awaits a future fulfillment. What nation of the Earth today has the national emblem of the great eagle? America is the nation that has the national emblem of the great eagle.

The context of the apocalypse is dealing with nations. The United Nations, perhaps appointed America, and America has been Israel's one ally throughout history since 1948.

The process of elimination brings us to the fact that the two wings of the eagle must be America. The King of the North is Russia. The King of the South is Egypt.

The Context Is Future

The events of this chapter in the book of Revelation, the apocalypse of the New Testament, have never happened. Further, a comparison to chapter 17, shows by a transfer of power from the dragon, the beast receives the dragon's authority, power, and rule. The beast is supported by ten horns and sevens heads.

These seven heads are plainly interpreted for us in Revelation 17 as seven mountains. The ten horns are a group of ten kings who support the beast, the Anti-Christ. The hour has not come when they will receive their kingdom and power of rule.* The seven heads are also seven religious kings.

Zechariah 12-14

In this context, all nations are gathered together against Israel under U.N. sanction. Israel's refusal to give up her land has brought U.N. enforcement. America is implied in the "all nations" gathered against Israel.*

*Revelation 17:9;17:12; N.W. Mathers, *The New Beyond,* p.74

The economic hardship in Russia is real because the party has taken it all for themselves leaving the people to face severe economic hardships. It often seems that the Russian party has left the task of feeding and caring for their people to America.

The Bible on Russia in the end time scriptures such as Daniel 11:40-43 and 11:44 combined with Ezekiel 38 & 39 document the military might of the King of the North. Russia has three complete armies on the battle field during the battles of Armageddon.

The Good News

God has not decreed that Russia will ever become a world empire, but rather a world power. What is the difference? A world empire will rule the world. A world power will be a super-power along with other superpower nations.

How do we know that God has not decreed Russia to be a world empire? The divine decree of God outlining world history for us found in Daniel, chapters 2 & 7 has not included Russia among the world empires. God's decree before the world began called for these powers to become world empires - Babylon, Medio-Persia, Greece, Rome, the revived Roman Empire, and Christ's millennial kingdom. The Millennium will yet come upon the earth for a period of 1000 years. Won't it be great to live for ten life times?

STUDY QUESTIONS

1. What modern day nations are to be found in Ezekiel 38 & 39?
2. What relationship does Tarshish have to Noah's three sons?
3. What is America's defense against aggression and invasion on the part of the nations in the end times?
4. Where is America to be found in the book of Revelation?
5. Who is the woman in Revelation, chapter 12?
6. What nation is the two wings of the great eagle in the book of Revelation?
7. Why are the two wings of the eagle America?
8. Who is the King of the North? Who is the King of the South?
9. What second reference is made to America in Zechariah, chapters 12-14?
10. What is the difference between a world empire and a world power?

3

THE BALANCE OF POWER

Those interested in the question of whether America is in prophecy must understand the end time power blocks.

The King Of The North

Russia is declared the King of the North in the Bible. The Russian power block has the strength to maneuver three Russian armies on the battlefield in the end times.*

Russian Propaganda

In our day, Russian propaganda has been spread to the effect that Russia has collapsed economically and is no longer a danger to America. The cold war is over and America need not be armed as previously was the case during the cold war. This is the author's opinion on the present day thinking which is abroad in our land.

The Great Military Might Of Russia

Yet, the Bible speaks of the great military might and power of Russia in the last days prior to the second coming of Christ.

In Your Opinion, What Has Happened?

Given the predictions of the Bible of the Russian power and might in the end times, the party is still ruling Russia with an iron fist. The opening and apparent freedom in Russia is real but is being controlled by the party. Much of what is happening in Russia is to deceive the western world, I believe. The party is directing its energy and time to a continuing military build-up of army and weapons with the goal of global rule.

Babylon, Medio-Persia, Greece, Rome are world empires that have run their course and have fallen. The revived or reshaped Roman Empire and Christ's millennial kingdom are yet future world empires.

America In Prophecy

If one insists on chapter and verse to establish the definite role of America in Prophecy, the only scripture predicting America's end time role is that given in chapter 2 of our book. However, the chapter and verse idea for everything in the Bible is a very poor method to establish a working theology. Those wanting a chapter and verse for every view from the Bible may not know that the Bible was not originally written in chapters and verses. The Bible was written in paragraphs. If you want to establish the role of America in end time events then you must argue or reason within the divine framework of prophecy established in the Bible. A lot of views on America have been largely common knowledge and shared seed thoughts. The need is for the development of the role of America in prophecy argued within the prophetic framework that we have in the Bible. *Beyond Our Time* seeks to do just that to present the argument for the role of America in end time events within the prophetic frame.

Future World Power - A Reshaped Roman Empire

The Bible predicts that a new world power, a world empire is not too far off and will soon come about in Europe.

Daniel On Rome

Daniel predicted the revival of the Roman empire back in the 6th century B.C. during the Babylonian captivity. The revival of Rome is based on the meaning behind the toes of the statue.*

*Daniel, Chapter 2

It is during the days of these kings who form the new Roman empire that the God of heaven will bring about another kingdom. This new kingdom will crush all other kingdoms and endure forever.*

*Daniel, Chapter 2

The Smiting Stone?

This stone which is prepared without hands is Jesus Christ. The smiting stone strikes the statue at its feet, completely crushing it. These world empires represented by the various metals were ground to dust.

The Kingdom Filled The Earth

The stone that struck the statue became a great mountain and this great mountain encompassed the entire earth.

World Dictator

Daniel spoke further of a world dictator who is yet to be revealed. He is referred to as "the little horn."

This is an interesting figure of speech. Every time we look on a certain American dollar bill, the eye looks at us from the pyramid.

The world dictator arises out of Rome's reshaped empire, the United States of Europe. In Daniel, the little horn has the eyes of a man and a mouth that speaks great swelling words.

My point is that the revived Roman Empire will be the second major power block on the earth during the tribulation period. The King of the North, Russia, will be a major power block on the earth during this time. The Bible predicts a third major power block on the earth: the Kings of the East, China and the Orient.

The Argument To Date

Beyond Our Time seeks to develop the major idea that the role of America in prophecy can be understood as one argues within a prophecy framework. The prophecy framework is the times and the seasons established by God before the foundation of the world and recorded accurately in the Bible. The chapter and verse method will not help establish the same certainty in understanding the role of America in prophecy as establishing America's role from the known prophecy framework that we have in the Bible. The second chapter of *Beyond Our Time* gives the chapter and verses that point to the presence of America in the end times.

While everyone may have an opinion on America in prophecy which forms a sort of common knowledge, it remains just that - mere opinion. The need is for a prophetic book that develops as fully as possible this question of America in prophecy.

The King Of The South

Egypt is known in the Bible as the king of the south. This old biblical nation will support Russia in the end times. The Arab-African power block, including the P.L.O., will fight on the side of Russia.

Western World Power

Western world power will be transferred during the final events of the last days to Europe. This global shift in the economic and political power and might of Europe is beginning to take shape before our eyes. While perception is not always knowledge but sense perception, the eyes of our world are turning to and envying Europe.

NAFTA

It is often difficult to make the right decision. In this author's opinion, NAFTA was a bad mistake on the part of America. NAFTA can only add to America's decline. American goods will be priced out of the market in the majority of areas, unable to compete with world competitors. In our day when the market is a global one, this is a serious mistake that can only add greatly to our economic problems at home.

United States of Europe

The Bible predicts clearly that the little horn, the beast, the anti-christ known by the number 666 will be supported by a united kingdom, referred to in Daniel and Revelation as a ten-king confederacy. The book of Revelation in the New Testament adds additional light to the book of Daniel. The dragon, Revelation tells us, supports the beast during his period of world rule.*

*Daniel 7:24; Revelation 9, 13, 16, 17 and 19; Daniel 11:40-44.

America - Super Power

America has enjoyed the shift in the balance of power during the twentieth century. America has been a world enforcer of the principles of law and order throughout the earth. America has stood as a nation for human rights and decency against the aggression and unrighteous actions of other countries of the world.

World Power

During the 70th week of Daniel, world power will be centered in Europe. Eventually, once Christ comes back and puts down the armies of the earth, during the final battle of Armageddon, world rule and power will be centered in Jerusalem.*

*Revelation, 19:11-21.

The Chinese are another major military block of power that both Daniel and Revelation predict during the final events of the end times.

John predicts the Chinese have a human wave army of 200 million. Earlier in Revelation, they kill a third of the earth's population.

America Is In Prophecy

At present, the divine clock is stopped. The clock begins to tick when the world dictator, the Antichrist and the world ecumenical church force a peace treaty on Israel. The author believes at the present time, although Revelation ceased with the completion of the canon in 90 A.D., the Lord God is showing us things to come in a non-revelatory sense. I mean by this that current events in our day will be the real thing during the tribulation period. The idea of a peace covenant with Israel by the western political and religious power of that day is found in the Bible predictions of our future.*

*Daniel 9:7; Maxwell S. Coder, *Jesus Is Coming,* on I, II Kings.

The King Principle

The welfare, prosperity, the state of America is largely due to the leadership of its president. This principle can be compared to the kings of Israel and Judah during the periods of bible history known as the united, divided and single kingdoms.

The walk of the king in the books of I, II Kings in the Bible, the king's morality and relationship with God determined the length of his rule, also the conditions of the nation and the quality of life under the king.

Likewise a strong American president will lead his country and those citizens under his leadership to enjoy greater bliss, economic prosperity and a healthy nation. A divine principle in scripture is that the ruler is directly responsible to God as seen in the kings of Israel and Judah.

While it is true that it was under a different dispensation, righteousness and righteous rule always exalt a nation. Corruption burdens the nation and the people.*

*Proverbs 14:34

Partial Conclusion

America is in prophecy end time events. The chapter and verse method will not help us understand the role that America plays in the end times. Some scripture is available as developed in chapter 2 that predicts America's actions during the tribulation period. Many have the common knowledge that is held in America in prophecy.

The historical method whereby we establish a frame of reference to argue the event and its time from within the prophetic framework is probably the best approach to fully developing our understanding of America in prophecy. An interpretation of the event and time frame reference is given based on the framework established. A philosophy or philosophical belief will follow on America in prophecy.

Biblical Framework

Our framework for the discussion of America in prophecy is based on the Bible's prophecies of the end times. While the many ideas on America in prophecy are often personal opinions, the need is for a book that fully develops America in prophecy based on reason from the scriptures.

STUDY QUESTIONS

1. What concept must be understood in the study of the time of the end?
2. How is the role of America established in bible prophecy other than the direct biblical references?
3. What end time power blocks are seen in the Bible?
4. Why can we be proud of our country?
5. How does the 70th week of Daniel aid our understanding of the time of the end?
6. What truth does the biblical principle of Proverbs 14:34 convey in the life of a nation?
7. What is the best approach to fully develop our understanding of America in bible prophecy?
8. What two things follow from the establishment of a prophetic framework to understand America in prophecy?

4

SILENCE

Others have thought that America is destroyed by an atomic war or other catastrophe. This is said to be an argument from silence. Therefore, America has no longer a voice in international affairs.

Prophets and prophecies outside of the Bible speak of the destruction of America.

Rene Noorbergen predicted the third world war is to be fought here at home on American soil. In July 1999, according to Noorbergen, the great king of terror will be back with vengeance for the earth. The reign of terror will be brought in by the king of terror.

Understanding America In Prophecy

To understand the role of America in prophecy, we must grasp the meaning of Revelation, chapter 13 as it relates to world prophetic events.

The thirteenth chapter of Revelation contributes to our understanding of the role of America in end time events. Examining Revelation 13 will help us to test the idea as to what the role of America is in prophecy.

The Role Of America In Prophecy

The western super power of the future will be the reshaped Roman Empire. The head of the roman power block will be the beast. He is known in the Bible as the Antichrist. His authority will extend over the realm of the political, religious, social, and economic spheres. The beast is supported by a religious figure called the false prophet.

The whole world worships the beast whose death wound has been healed. The world dictator has the authority, power, and wisdom of the dragon. He brings to life the revived (reshaped) Roman empire. Many through the ages have tried to do this but it is reserved for the Antichrist. The whole world will go after the beast believing the lie that the Antichrist is God.

What Is The Death Wound?

The death wound was not a fatal blow to his head but the death of the old Roman Empire. The healing of the death wound is the beast's ability to put together and bring to life the old Roman Empire.

An Idolatrous Statue

An idolatrous statue of the first beast is erected. The religious beast causes the image of the Antichrist to come to life. Those on the earth who do not worship the image will be killed.

The Mark Of The Beast

All of humanity living at that time must receive the new universal identification code the number 666 either on their forehead or on their right hand. They will not be able to buy or sell without the mark of the beast.*
*Revelation 13:1-18.

The Second Beast

This religious figure brings worship to the political beast. He causes the earth to worship the beast. The religious beast has two horns like a lamb. The Bible draws attention to the fact that he was speaking as a dragon.

Great Signs

The religious breast is able to perform great miracles before men. Fire falls from heaven. The prophet deceives the earth with the belief that the Antichrist is God.

The Antichrist rules by power, authority and wisdom given to him by the dragon.

The Beast's Political Kingdom

Both Daniel and Revelation, the books that contribute much to our prophetic understanding reveal that the Antichrist is supported by a western European confederacy of ten kings.*
*Daniel 7:24; Revelation 13:1;17:12-13; Daniel 9:27; Revelation 17:3-5-8.

America Is Not The Superpower That It Is Today

America will not be the superpower that it is today during the end times. The Antichrist, the religious figure, and the ten kings will be the western superpower of that day during the tribulation period.

The Real Peace Treaty

The revived Roman Empire which includes the political beast, the ten nation superpower, and the world church will force a peace accord with Israel at the beginning of that final seven year period. No mention of America is made as the western superpower of the end times. Rather, the United States of Europe is the western superpower of the end times.

America may be one of the ten kings found in the books of Daniel and Revelation. The superpower of the end times is the revived Roman Empire and the Roman political leader.

Isn't This An Argument From Silence?

Often, since it is not stated that America is a super power during the end times, many misconstrue that no mention of America means that nothing can be said about the subject. This is an argument from silence to argue that America is not to be found in the end times of bible prophecy.

Does It Say Who The Western Superpower Will Be?

The fact that the Bible is clear on the western superpower of that day must mean, at the very least, that America is not the superpower of that day.

What Are The Possibilities?

The real possibility is that America which we dearly love will be submitted to this world ruler with his one-world government, bank and economy. Worshiped as God, the Roman beast brings in a reign of peace and prosperity for 3½ years.

The Rule Of The Roman Political Leader

The rule of the Roman leaders and the western super-kings of end times is no argument from silence. They are the western superpower of that day rather than any other western power.

Bible scholar, Dr. J. F. Walvoord points out that since the descendants of America come mostly from the British Isles and Europe that America would identify with the western ruler and his kingdom.*

*J.F. Walvoord, *The Nations in Prophecy*, p. 173.

Decline

America, though continuing as a nation, will have declined in power as evidenced by the superpower of the west predicted to rule over the earth in the end times. It should be pointed out that America could well be one of the ten kings that support the beast and his political-religio-economic kingdom.

Those who argue that the silence of the Bible on the subject of America are begging the question. The Bible states very positively that the western superpower of the day will be the Roman leader and Roman kingdom. This means that no other western power can be the western superpower of that day. We need to focus positively on what the Bible says and the revelation that we have rather than what we do not have on the subject of America in prophecy.

STUDY QUESTIONS

1. Why is the argument that America will be destroyed by an atomic war not valid?
2. What prophets and prophecies outside of the Bible speak of the destruction of our beloved America?
3. To understand the role of America in prophecy, what prophetic understanding must be grasped?
4. What does Revelation chapter 13 tell us about the eastern superpower of the future?
5. What is the death wound of the new world leader?
6. Who is the second beast?
7. In Satan's theocracy, who will be the two rulers?
8. Who are the ten horns of Daniel and Revelation?
9. How do the ten horns differ from the seven heads seen in Revelation chapter 17?
10. Who makes the real peace treaty with Israel?
11. Who are the superpowers of the end times?
12. If America is not the western superpower of the end time then what are the possibilities?
13. Why would America identify with the western superpower and super kings?

5

WILL AMERICA BE DESTROYED BY NUCLEAR ATTACK?

Nuclear Destruction

I was asked recently on a radio talk show whether America would be destroyed by a nuclear war. This is one of the thoughts that people have on America in prophecy. Since we have entered the nuclear age in the 90's, such thinking is justified.

A nuclear attack is a real possibility. The Cuban missile crisis of the early 60's was Russia's way of keeping America out of Cuba. It is very possible that a nuclear attack may occur against America before the Rapture of the church.

Wars And Insurrections

Jesus told us that before his second coming, kingdom will be raised against kingdom.*
*Luke 21

It is a very real possibility that the current wave of violence may continue to intensify ending with another major crisis at the end of the century.

Historical Examples

The Roman republic fell. While the republic lasted some four hundred years, the day came when the Roman empire was sacked by foreign powers.

What Contributed To The Fall Of The Roman Empire?

A vast number of books have been written on the fall of the Roman Empire. The eastern part of the empire continued until the year 1453 A.D.; the western part of the Roman Empire, with its capital at Rome, collapsed.

Rome's Two Basic Problems

The Roman Empire had two basic problems that caused its downfall. The first was a defense problem whereby it ceased to be able to defend its borders. Secondly, it developed a series of internal problems from which the nation was never able to recover. The late F. F. Bruce in his book, "The Spreading Flame", suggests, in addition to the defense problem, an excessive bureaucracy developed by Diocletian.

Fallen, Fallen Is Babylon The Great

Rome, having fallen, was invaded and sacked a number of times beginning in 410 A.D. with Alaric. Robert S. Hoyt in his work *"Europe In The Middle Ages"* agrees with the common opinion of scholarly consensus that defense was the number one problem of the Roman Empire leading to its downfall.

Trade And Industry At A Standstill

Nothing was moving! Money was hoarded by the many due to the uncertainty of the future. Others invested very heavily particularly in land. The middle-class was suffering from their inability to sell their goods or their services. Money became very tight and the costs of goods and services were deflated. These internal economic problems dealt a death blow to the Roman economy.*
  *Earle E. Cairns, *Christianity Through The Centuries,* pp 169-170

Government Re-Organized

Hoyt points out further that Constantine and those who came after him tried to reorganize the government. Strangely enough, the considerable laws and measures that were enacted brought disaster that much sooner.

Problems In Their Cities

The Roman Empire developed a series of problems within its cities that contributed as well to its fall.*
  *Earle E. Cairns, *Christianity Through The Centuries,* pp 169-170

Heavy Taxation

The burden of heavy taxation to support the Roman Empire and its bureaucracy fell upon the shoulders of the lower classes.

Weakened, Weakened Is Babylon The Great

Rome fell prey to the barbarians, the German tribes, the Goths and the Huns. Attila was thought by many to be the scourge of God. Earle E. Cairns in his work *"Christianity Through The Centuries"* points out that one of the clerical leaders of that day talked Attila into stopping his looting and destruction of Rome.

In Our Day

As we have considered some major problems that brought down Rome, one can no doubt see parallels to our own day. The defense problem, coupled with serious economic problems and internal problems particularly in the cities of the Roman Empire led to the fall of the west.

The shift in power is returning to Europe. Europe is working feverishly for a unification by the end of the century. A one common defense and currency to prepare Europe for her world leader, the Antichrist.

STUDY QUESTIONS

1. Why is speculative thinking on a nuclear attack against America justified?
2. What contributed to the fall of the Roman Republic?
3. What specific problems in the Roman Empire parallel the problems of our day?
4. What is the goal of present day European unification?

6

WHY DOES AMERICA REMAIN?

America is an enigma to some who suggest that the reason that America remains is because this country as no other nation has been blessed of God. This is a fine patriotic argument but should be recognized for what it is, patriotism. Patriotism is good and America is a wonderful country.

Forms Of The Patriotic Argument

Others see America remaining because no other country supports the gospel cause, the missionary activity, and Christian churches as does America.

Rome Had Her Christians

The Early Church had the ministry, presence and guidance of the apostles. The early church was a dynamic church as seen by the inspired historical account of its activities, the book of Acts. Yet Rome fell as a nation!

God Has Seen Fit To Spare America

Yes, some argue God has seen fit to spare America for one reason or another at the present time. On a Seattle radio interview, the suggestion was made that America has been blessed because of the treatment of the Jew.

The Promise Of God

Yes, God promised Abraham that he would bless those that blessed the Jew and curse those who treated the Jews badly.*
*Genesis 12
America has welcomed Jews and rightly so with all other legal immigrants giving them a great opportunity to earn a wonderful living.

Prosperous People

Many American Jews have been able to help Israel. While every presidency has had their policy towards the political structure of Israel and Jewish aspirations, America has welcomed and blessed the Jewish people with wonderful treatment.

God's Sovereignty

The next chapter on God's decree entitled "It's Fixed" is a chapter that the author hopes the reader will enjoy greatly. America has been blessed. It continues and is protected by the sovereign hand of God. God has made from one blood all nations that dwell on the face of the earth. Their times and their allotment of land is predetermined by the sovereign God.*
* Deuteronomy 32:8; Acts 17:26.
God has marked out and predestinated the length of days for nations and also their dwelling boundaries. America will continue as long as God has predestinated her life span to be.

The Sheep And The Goats' Judgement

All nations will be judged based on their treatment of the Jew during the tribulation. This is based on the sheep and goats judgement found in Matthew 25:31-46. They evidenced their faith by their works as seen in the treatment of Jewish Christians who were persecuted and without the necessities of life during the tribulation period.*
*Matthew 25:31-46.

America In The Sheep And The Goats' Judgement

America as a nation will face judgement at the end of the tribulation period for their treatment of these Jewish Christians during the tribulation. The sheep and goats' judgement will occur prior to the millennium. It will determine one's right to enter the millennium or to be cast into hell.

STUDY QUESTIONS

1. What is the meaning of the argument that America is blessed of God?
2. What are other forms of the patriotic argument?
3. Was the course of America's history predetermined? (What scriptures point to the predetermined decree of God?)
4. What arguments are the best Christian arguments of America being blessed by God?
5. What is the one certain argument for America being blessed by God in relationship to the Jew?
6. What will be the basis of America's judgement during the tribulation period?
7. If America continues to favor Israel and treat Israel well now and throughout the tribulation period, what conclusion can we draw?

7

IT'S FIXED!

Of Course America Is In Prophecy, America Exists!

The plan of God found in Acts 17:22-34 has much to contribute to our thinking of America in prophecy.

The Plan Of God

The sovereignty of God means God is the supreme ruler. God is drawing the age to a close summing up and concluding all things in Christ.. (Eph. 1:10)

All Things

All things are working according to His eternal plan based on infinite mind and will.*
*(Eph. 1:11)

Nations Predetermined By God

When Paul addressed the philosophers at Mar's Hill, he stated very clearly that the duration of the nations and their boundaries are predetermined by God.

The Father has predetermined their seasons and points of rule of the nations in time.*
*(Acts 17:26)

The eternal decree of God planned, fixed, and predetermined the boundaries of the nations before the world began.

What Does This Mean?

All nations are given by God a period of reign time and the extent of their boundaries and influence is also predetermined by God.

* Charles Hodge, *Systematic Theology*, Vol. 1, p 144.

When Did This Happen?

In the eternal plan of God, God planned, fixed, and determined before the world began. Further, Daniel 2 & 7 tell us that God has predetermined the number and succession of world empires. There is a difference between a world empire and a world power.

Why Has He Done It?

Why has God preplanned, fixed and predetermined their point in time of the rule of the nations and their boundaries.

In the Greek text, Acts 17:27 should be read with Acts 17:26 so that the nations will seek God.*

*Acts 17:26-27.

Is It Fair?

Yes, because the infinite omniscience and wisdom of God are behind his eternal plan. God's omniscience extends to all things both actual and realized.*

* Matthew 11:20-24.

Summary

God has fixed the duration given to each nation both in terms of their time of rule and also in terms of their boundary allotment. He has done this so that the nations will seek him.

STUDY QUESTIONS

1. Of course, America is in prophecy. What does Acts 17:22-34 contribute to our thinking about America in prophecy?
2. What two key factors in the life of a nation are predetermined by God?
3. When did God the Father predetermine the two factors concerning the life of a nation?
4. What is the meaning of Ephesians chapter one verse eleven?
5. Why has God fixed the duration and boundaries of the nations?
6. Is it Fair?
7. What message does Matthew 11:20-24 convey?

8

THE TIMES AND THE SEASONS

Born Again

What will happen to America? The question of what will happen to the nation in prophecy is largely a question of what will happen to the evangelical population within America. The fundamentalists who may not be evangelicals and whose battle cry of the faith is found in Jude 3 have to be included in the born from above population.

What Does This Mean?

The born-again population in America will be raptured prior to the tribulation period. The certainty of the Rapture prior to the tribulation period, a seven year period, of divine judgement on the earth is found in I Thess. 4:13-5:11.

The Holy Spirit Withdrawn

The Bible tells us that the Holy Spirit is the restrainer of the flood gates of evil.*
* 2 Thess. 2:6.
After the church is withdrawn then the man of sin will be revealed.*
*2 Thess. 2:7-8.
America will be part of the world left behind after the Rapture of the church.

Reverse Pattern

The Spirit of God took up His residence in the church on the day of Pentecost. Those who have trusted Christ as savior and been born again will suddenly be called home at the Rapture of the church.

The Spirit of God will be withdrawn from indwelling the church when the church is raptured. The reversal of the divine pattern on the day of Pentecost will occur at the Rapture of the church.*
* I Thess. 4:13-18.

The Mystery of Lawlessness

Paul tells us that the mystery of lawlessness which began in his day is at work.*
* 2 Thess. 2:7.

The completion of the mystery of lawlessness will be the revelation of the man of sin, the Antichrist.

Is the Rapture a Biblical Teaching?

The Rapture is tied to the gospel, and is part of the gospel. I Thess. 4:14 is a first class condition in the Greek language that assumes the reality of the fact. If we believe that Jesus died and rose again and we do (says Paul) then the ones having been put to sleep through Jesus, God will bring with him.*
Greek New Testament, I Thess. 4:14.

Are You Sure, Paul?

The apostle states that we say this by the word of the lord. The word Lord is in the genitive case and is a genitive of source. Paul received a special revelation from the lord on this subject.

The question what will happen to our loved ones who have died in Christ before the Lord's return has been answered by Paul.

When Is The Rapture?

Without any warning, suddenly the Lord will appear in the air with the command.*
*I Thess. 4:16.
As the commander of the saints, He will give the command for the troops to move out.*
*I Thess. 4:16-17.
Those who have died in Christ and those who are alive will go up, together, in the air to meet the Lord.
Keep on comforting one another with these words!*
* I Thess. 4:18.

Not Destined For Wrath

Paul states this very clearly in I Thessalonians 5:9 that the brethren (the church) are not destined for wrath. The context considered points to the time of wrath, the tribulation, the day of the Lord. The Old Testament name for the judgement program of God on the earth was the day of the Lord.

God Himself has not appointed us to wrath but to obtaining salvation through our Lord Jesus Christ.*

* Greek New Testament, I Thess. 5:9.

The time of wrath spoken of in the context is the tribulation period of divine judgement, on the earth known as the day of the Lord.*

* Greek New Testament, I Thess. 5:9.

I Thess. 5:10-11

Paul restates the truth of the Rapture. Whether we have died in Christ or are alive at the Rapture of the church, we are going to be with Christ.*

But You Brethren Are Not In Darkness

The world those outside of Christ of which America is a part do not know what time it is on God's prophetic clock.

No Warning

The time of judgement from God will come on the earth without any warning.*

Any Clues

The cry of that generation upon which the day of the Lord's divine judgement will fall without any warning is given in I Thess. 5:3.

When They Cry Peace and Security

The cry for world peace and security is the cry of our generation. The Bible tells us that destruction will fall from heaven without any warning. The seal, trumpet, and bowl judgements of the book of Revelation are the sudden destructions.

America's Cry

America's cry is for peace and security. Americans want peace and security every bit as much as the rest of the world. Paul differentiates between the world and those born again in I Thessalonians 5:4. Those born again are indwelt by the Holy Spirit. These are the sons of light and of the day.*
* I Thess. 5:2.

America's Sons Of The Day

As sons of light, the Christian has a revelation, the divine prophecy plan of God for the ages, the Bible. They are not of the night or darkness but rather sons of the day. Our experience will be completely different than the experience of the world, who receive the day of divine retribution.

The best way to illustrate the time frame and reference that Paul has in mind is to explain the difference in weather usually between the south and the north in winter. The south may be receiving warm temperatures and sunshine with no snow. The north at the same time likely is receiving sub-zero temperatures: snow, sleet, and howling winds. While the church is raptured and taken to the Father's house, the world will be experiencing the judgements of God.

The World Of Which America Is Part

The earth will be receiving the divine retribution reserved for her in the book of Revelation. Yes, America will form part of the population left behind at the Rapture of the church. Her born again population gone, America will experience the events of the Day of the Lord.

* I Thess. 5:5: John 14:2-3

In The Meantime

Christians ought to pray for their leaders, pay our taxes, and live in civil obedience and loyalty to the state. Since the state is the minister of God, the powers that be are ordained of God.*

*Romans 13:1-7.

STUDY QUESTIONS

1. What will happen to America?
2. What is the real question about America in prophecy?
3. What is the significance of clarification of this question?
4. A first class condition in the Greek language of I Thess. 4:14 means?
5. The Rapture occurs before the tribulation begins see I Thess. 5:9. What does this mean?
6. What does I Thess. 5:10-11 teach?
7. What are the two cries of man universally true prior to unexpected judgement on America?
8. The born again population gone, what will America experience?
9. What are Christians commanded to do in the meantime?

9

AMERICA IN THE POST CHRISTIAN ERA

Some have claimed that we are living in a post christian era. This line of argument claims that the Judaeo Christian tradition has been rejected by the nation.

Two Responses

The hard times that Paul predicted which began in his day pointed to a race motivated by love of self, money, and pleasure. So the race is motivated by devotion to self pursuits, money and pleasure to the exclusion of God*

* 2 Tim. 3:4.

The Greek New Testament gives an accurate reading to us that the translation should be lovers of pleasure to the exclusion of God. This is one of the major signs of the last days.

Difficult Days To Minister In

Ministry in such a day and age as well as living out the Christian life is difficult. America is characterized by a nation who are lovers of self, money and the pursuit of pleasure.

Belief And Unbelief

The Christian message brings two main responses one is belief and the other is unbelief.*
*2 Tim. 3:1-17.
This is the synthesis of the response of all humanity, not only America but also the human race.

Confirmed In Unbelief

If we understand the prophecy of Isaiah then we understand that Isaiah was sent to minister to a society that was ready and ripe for judgement. The divine discipline came in 722 B.C. when the Lord God raised up a national enemy against Israel. The ten northern tribes fell to Assyria in 722 B.C.

The Assyrians left some Israelites in the land and brought Assyrians to live in the land of Israel. The offspring of the intermarriage of the Jews and Assyrians were the Samaritans.

A National Crisis

Look for national crises in the major western nations in the future! It was in the year of a national crisis, Isaiah received his call and commission to Israel. The revelation helped Isaiah understand that his mission was to confirm Israel in unbelief.*
* Isaiah 6:11.

Isaiah wanted to know when can I get a new job. Notice Isaiah's response "When can I get out of this mess!" This was because the Lord God earlier told Isaiah that the generation to whom he was to minister wouldn't listen to a thing that he had to say.

Jesus Picked Up This Passage In the Parables

In Matthew 13, the Lord explained to his disciples why he taught in parables. As God, He hid the truth from his hearers so as not to bring them into any greater judgement than they had already incurred due to His rejection by the nation.

Isaiah's Israel Hardened

The ten northern tribes had become hardened. They were given over the position known as scoffers. Israel had made a pact or covenant with hell. They had turned to black magic and believed that Assyria, the scourge of God would not reach them.*
*Isaiah 28:1-29.

The Parallel To Our Day The Point Of No Return

There is a point known only to God where a nation passes the point of no return. Isaiah's argument reveals that Israel had forsaken the Lord. They had substituted for a right relationship with God.* The Lord God had abandoned Israel temporarily.*
*Isaiah 1:10-31; Isaiah 2:5-11.

The Economy Struck Down

The Lord God struck their economy. The message over and over in the prophets, a theme of the prophets, was that the Lord God struck the nation again and again.

Particularly, the crops became centers of catastrophic judgement and failure because of divine judgement. Long periods of draught were used as a disciplining agent against Israel and Judah.

Yet They Wouldn't Repent

One of the well known lines of the prophets sticks with me so well: "Rend your hearts and not your garments!" Israel Wouldn't Repent!

That's right, Israel didn't repent, so the Lord used Assyria as the disciplining rod to end the history of Israel's northern kingdom as it was then known in 722 B.C.

Judah Learned Idolatry

The sin of idolatry was the sin that destroyed Israel. Judah learned the sin of idolatry from Israel. Idolatry became such a snare to the nation that eventually the Lord God raised up the Babylonians as the disciplining agent to take Judah captive to Babylon for 70 years.

How Long Does America Have Left As A Nation?

We are living in a different dispensation so that God may spare America divine judgement until the Rapture. Read my argument of the question of America's continuation as a nation based on Romans 9.

In this dispensation of grace, which began on the day of Pentecost and ends at the Rapture of the church, it is possible that we could face destruction, or be conquered by another people. Such is the possible human experience of nations within the history of the race, and the world. I believe that my argument based on Romans 9 has some good news that it is a biblical argument, and analogy that shows clearly God will spare America until the Rapture of the church.

STUDY QUESTIONS

1. What are the two major signs of the approaching destruction of the Day of the Lord?
2. How will the Day of the Lord break upon America?
3. What do the words "peace when there is no peace" mean?
4. What parallel can be drawn between Judah and Jerusalem of the period of the single kingdom (721-586 B.C.) and America today?
5. Why did the false prophets cry peace?

10

AMERICA AT PRESENT

The Defense Question

The defense question is one of the key factors in our preservation as a people. Internally, our ability to solve our problems in the cities and anarchy and terrorism at home. The military, and the trade problem are props that are holding our nation together. America's inability to compete on the market both at home and abroad has grave consequences for the American people. Unemployment, inability to create jobs leads to a frustrated and disappearing middle class.

Economic Problems Breed Violence

The inability of any people to solve their economic and domestic problems paves the way for unrest on an individual, domestic, and national level.

NAFTA- A Dreadful Mistake

A mistake in economic dealing is the NAFTA idea. Americans should not be made to compete at home with foreign competitors who produce goods more cheaply than do Americans.

Americans may not be able to produce goods at a competitive price with foreign goods. A free trade agreement means Americans cannot sell their goods. This causes cuts, scale downs, layoffs, in the market place. Economic problems and problems for our society are bound to mushroom!

Automobiles can be produced cheaper outside of America than in America.

The Folly Of The Hour

America is entering into free trade agreements with parts of the world.

Tariffs

Tariffs may not make that much difference because the cheaper produced goods with tariffs may be still a much lower price than that which is produced in America. Cheap is not always best but in a tight economy, price often does become one of the key factors in determining purchases. The question of quality while crucial at home may not make much difference when comparison is made to foreign goods.

NAFTA Means One World Order

The need that is maintained for such things as NAFTA must stem from the idea of a new world order.

While a western power block of ten nations headed by a western dictator is the western power block of Bible prophecy, the present time America must maintain her identity and separateness from other nations.

At the present time all schemes to fit America into a one world order should be scrapped since this will occur after the Rapture of the church.*

* 2 Thessalonians 2:3-12.

Is The Church Apostate At The Present Time?

America is the great missionary and gospel preaching nation. This is partially true and can be verified by church history. Yet the Bible predicts in the last days that the church will not endure sound doctrine.*

* 2 Timoth 4:1-8.

Instead, the Christian church of the end times will be turned to myths. They will accumulate teachers who can tickle their ears. In a real sense, the apostasy is with us at the present time.

The Church During The Tribulation

The saints will be on the outside looking in during the tribulation period. They will not be a part of the organized world church of that day. The important factors in the worship of the world church in the early part of the tribulation prior to it's destruction, will be those experiences and concepts not centered in biblical truth.*

* Revelation 17:16-18.

Conclusion

It is interesting to think that both Israel and Judah were disciplined by Assyria and Babylon respectively.

I heard a Russian army officer say recently on television that only a global war would restore the former Soviet Union. Nuclear war destroys, so this would seem to be a bit of a contradiction. The balance of power in the world at the present time is distributed between America, Russia and China. Russia and China are two distinct entities. An even more interesting question is to reflect upon the strength of Russia and China in the end times. Daniel 11 confirms the Russians are able to put three full armies on the battlefield during the battles of Armageddon.*

*Ezekiel 38 & 39; Daniel 11:40-44.

The incredible size and power of modern day China is awesome. China will play her part during the tribulation period. Remember, the tribulation period begins after the Rapture. The tribulation lasts seven years. Christ's second coming will be at the end of the seven year tribulation. He will set up His millennial kingdom and rule for a thousand years from Jerusalem.

The red Chinese will kill a third of all mankind during the last three and a half years of the tribulation.

A clear reference is made to the kings of the land of the going up of the sun. (Literal translation from the Greek New Testament) The great vast human wave army crosses the Euphrates and enters the holy land for this final battle.* The number of the army all riding on horses is two hundred million.*

*Revelation 9:15-16; Revelation 16:12-15.

No Mention Of America During The Battle Of Armageddon

The silence of the Bible on this all important question means that they are not a super power during the tribulation Armageddon battles. During the first battle of Armageddon, America gives verbal political rhetoric and rebuke to the advancing Russian army invading Israel.*

*Ezekiel 38:10-13

Likely the fact that America is given to the love of self, money and pleasure during the last days accounts for the decline of our beloved nation.

Our Prayer Should Be God Spare America

We are instructed in the Bible to pray for our leaders that an atmosphere of stability may prevail for the spread of the gospel. The day of grace and the age of grace will draw to an end when the trumpet of the Lord calls the church home!

If America was a super power during the tribulation then it would be stated during the battles of Armageddon. The silence of the Bible on the role of America must be interpreted as America's decline in power. This would seem a fair, reasonable logical and rational deduction to be made based on the Bible's revelation of end time power blocks.

STUDY QUESTIONS

1. What disciplining agents has God raised up against America?
2. What is the purpose of God striking any nation?
3. How long has America left as a nation?
4. How does Romans 9 help us understand the role of God for America?
5. What problems does America face at present?
6. What is the best course politically for America to follow at present?
7. In the last days, Paul predicted in 2 Timothy 4, men will not endure sound doctrine. What does this mean? What should be our response?
8. Is the protestant church apostate now or during the tribulation? Or Both?

11

AMERICA'S SEAL JUDGEMENTS

The seal judgements which fall on America during the tribulation are predicted in Revelation 6.

Rainbows - Rainbows

The lamb, Jesus Christ, delivers the earth into the hands of this Roman leader. The Roman ruler has the bow which is the false symbol of peace.*
* Revelation 6:1-2.
The head of the revived Roman empire goes forth with great ferociousness to conquer. What graphic language the Bible uses, remember that Caesar talked of coming, seeing, and conquering.

Two Additional Observations

The color of the horse upon which the Roman Caesar rides is a white steed. The Greek New Testament puts the emphasis on the adjective not the noun which is the second attribute position of the adjective. The picture painted is of a shining, brilliant white steed.

Stephanas - An Ecclesiastical Crown

The victor's crown is worn by the Roman beast as he goes forth conquering and with the purpose of conquering. America will be conquered by this totalitarian military dictator.

America as part of the earth must suffer at the hands of this false Christ. He brings a false peace to the earth to those whom he conquers.*

* Revelation 6:2.

Peace Taken From America

The red horse takes peace from the earth. Jesus Christ has broken seal number two. Men kill one another. The effects of this divine judgement have fallen on us to some extent at the present time in our cities.

The broad sword given to the rider on the red horse was the Roman broad sword. The effectiveness of this sword depended on its weight.*

* Revelation 6:3-4.

Inflation & Famine

The third seal judgement upon America is the black horse. This third judgement brings runaway inflation and famine at a level unparalleled in the history of America. It will take one's income each day to buy food. During the tribulation, a day's pay will only buy enough to eat for one day. Expensive wheat is compared with a less expensive grain, barley. Even today, the price of groceries continues to soar. Groceries seem to be the new gold. The dollar at home seems to buy less and less each day.*
* Revelation 6:5-6.

Pair Of Scales

The third rider on this horse has a pair of scales bringing divine justice to the earth. Increasing famine and shortage of food supplies is predicted to increase and accelerate during the time of Jacob's trouble upon America.

The Pale Horse

The fourth judgement to fall upon America is the pale horse. It's rider's name is called death.*
* Revelation 6:7-8

The weakened state of America is such that one-fourth of our population at that time will die.

These seal judgements of Revelation 6 upon America have their parallel with the judgements predicted by Jesus in Matthew 24.

Religious Persecution

Tribulation saints saved during the first 3½ years of the tribulation period have been killed because of the word of God and their witness.

The state during this time under the Roman beast martyrs Christians for their faith in Jesus Christ. Those who were killed in the persecution of the Roman ruler are still alive. Their souls live on.

Cries To God

They are crying out to God, Jesus Christ, for Him, the sovereign ruler to avenge them! Retribution to those who are dwelling on the earth! White robes, and a time to rest is given to these modern martyrs.

Under The Roman Ruler

Under the beast, the Roman Ruler, the gospel will no longer be tolerated in America. The message of the 144,000 Jewish evangelists will be proclaimed in America.

The 144,000

A great multitude from America will respond to the message of these Jewish Evangelists.*
*Revelation 7:9-17.

Earthquake

Given the seriousness of California earthquakes of the recent past, the Bible points to a great earthquake, yet future in America.*
* Revelation 6:12-17.

Signs Appear In The Heavens

Yes, signs appear in the heavens at this future time, bringing untold suffering and instability to America. The sun becomes darkened. It will be cold during those days on the earth. The full moon appeared as covered with blood. The moon at times even in our present day appears to be covered with blood. The permanence of creation is being removed during these times of strange signs in the heavens.

Jesus Spoke About All This

Men's hearts will fail them for fear. Men will die from heart attacks due to fear.*
* Luke 21:25-26.
Falling stars! The sky is ripped apart. Mountains and islands are rearranged due to earthquakes.*
* Revelation 6:12-17.
All of these seal judgements are part of God's future judgement of America.

When Will This Take Place?

The seal judgements are simultaneous upon America lasting for forty two months.

When The Peace Treaty Is Signed

Once the peace treaty between the Roman ruler, Israel and world ecclesiastical body has been signed, the seal judgements will fall on America*
   * Revelation 6:2: 6:3-17.

STUDY QUESTIONS

1. What will America suffer during the seal judgements?
2. What shortages are predicted during the time of Jacob's trouble on the earth?
3. America and the pale horse, what does this judgement mean?
4. When will the gospel no longer be tolerated in America?
5. How long will America experience the seal judgements?
6. When will the seal judgements break forth upon America?

12

AMERICA IN THE MIDDLE EAST

Operation Desert Storm

Desert storm was an attention getter! Suddenly, the whole world's attention focused on the Middle East. American forces were headed to the Middle East.

Desert storm proved that the Middle East was no longer a regional conflict. This was a mini-Armageddon. Another interesting point was that here was an old biblical nation Babylon, modern day Iraq confronting modern man.

The figure of Saddam Hussein presented a complex figure. What were we to make of Saddam, another Hitler? Is Saddam the same personality and problem that the west faced with Hitler? The world was no longer a safe place, Saddam's presence brought the danger of global nuclear destruction.

Many Asked, Is This Armageddon?

Saddam Hussein, and the Kuwaiti-Iraqi invasion brought a test to America. Was the revolution testing American response to a nuclear threat?

The Peace Accord

What were we to make of that historic handshake on the white house lawn.? The Desert Storm fiasco brought home the reality that another disruption in the middle east could pull the whole world towards war.

It is not surprising in the least that a Middle East peace idea came out of desert storm. One talk show host asked me: "When you saw them shake hands on the White house lawn, what did you think?"

An unrealistic and over-enthusiastic optimism began to spread throughout America. Few people realized that as they shook hands on the White house lawn that the peace accord was only a great idea.

Russia In The Middle East

As I saw on television, the Russian official standing between Mr. Peres and the late Prime Minister Rabin, a symbolic message was presented to us who viewed by television.

Mr. Peres has been said to be an idealistic intellectual. The historic event on the white house lawn between the PLO's Arafat and Israel was at the very least a great idea. Would it work? All depended on Syria's Assad, he was the only one who could make the Middle East peace accord work. The peace accord would stand or fall depending on Syria's response.

Would Israel Exchange The Golan Heights For Peace With Syria?

It became clear as violence accelerated in the Gaza Strip, on the West bank, two of Arafat's top men were murdered, and others defected that it was a rip saw. All who grabbed hold of this would be ripped to pieces. Zechariah predicted that all who take up Jerusalem will reel.*
* Zechariah 12:1-3.

In The End Times

Jerusalem and Israel would become a millstone for all the people. Everyone who lifted it would be ground to bits.

Arafat's speech and behavior has not met with the expected norms both within the PLO and without.

Those who mess with Jerusalem according to Zechariah will severely injure themselves.*
* M. F. Unger, Zechariah, pp. 208-209

If the peace accord does go through, we are only a short time from a Russian invasion of Israel. Since Ezekiel 38:10-13 presents Israel swelling securely without any need for protection.

America's Role At The Present Time

America's secretary of state Warren Christopher tried to play the role of a mediator between the PLO and Israel.*
* U.S. News & World Report, 12/27/93-1/3/94, pp. 35-37 & p. 86.

America realizing the key role of Syria to the success or failure of the peace initiative is trying to mediate a peace agreement between Syria and Israel.

America exerts only a political rhetoric much in line with the American response to the future Russian invasion of Israel.

Why The Push For Peace In The Middle East?

Desert Storm proved that the conflict of the Middle East was no longer regional. Unchecked, the Middle East could explode all the world into war. The late Rabin's thinking was that a peace arrangement between Israel and Arab nations in the region is necessary before Iran becomes a nuclear power.*

Iran should be a nuclear power by the end of the century.

Israel will have to give back the Golan Heights to Syria in exchange for peace promises. Contemporary thinking which is common knowledge reports Syria is the leader of the pact. This takes the heat off of Egypt, the King of the South.

Is The Peace Accord In The Bible?

Does the Bible predict America will make this treaty with Israel, the PLO, and Syria? No; the Bible does not know of any such peace accord as was introduced in 1993.

The peace treaty referred to in Daniel Chapter 9 is not the peace accord initiative of 1993. The Roman ruler out of the revived Roman empire and with the world ecclesiastical body of that day will force a peace treaty on Israel. No, America is not the one to make this peace treaty with Israel.

While the PLO is found in the prophecy of Ezekiel, it is Syria who will form part of all Arabia. All Arabia is a Russian ally during the events of the end times.

STUDY QUESTIONS

1. What did the Desert Storm campaign prove?
2. What did Zechariah predict in Zechariah 12:1-3 about tries at all peace agreements?
3. What position has America taken towards Israel?
4. What particulars can we derive from the real peace treaty of Daniel Chapter 9?
5. When is the decline of America evident in Bible prophecy?

13

MYSTERY BABYLON THE GREAT

Fallen, Fallen Is Babylon*

Twelve times in the New Testament, the word Babylon is found. During the time of desert storm, one of the questions of interpretation that came up was the identity of Babylon. An error came about as to the fact that Babylon was Iraq.

Who, Then, Is Mystery Babylon?

Four times in Matthew, the captivity to Babylon is recorded whereby Babylon conquered the southern kingdom of Judah in 586 B.C. Stephen mentions Babylon in his defense to the official legal body of the day the Sanhedrin.**

* Revelation 17
**Acts 7:43

Peter in his first epistle, through Silvanus his amaneneuensis writes that the church in Babylon greets you as does John Mark.***

***I Peter 5:13.

A Strong Angel

A strong angel proclaims the fall of Babylon in Revelation 14:8. The seventh bowl judgement falls on Babylon in Revelation 16:19.

The Woman Riding Upon The Beast

In Revelation 17, The woman riding upon the beast is mystery Babylon, the great. Judgement falls on Babylon the great in Revelation 18. The great center of trade and commerce upon the earth is judged in this chapter of the Revelation. The kings of the earth stand at a distance watching Babylon burn.*

* Revelation 18:4-10.

The heavens are instructed to rejoice against Babylon who has been cast down by violence.*

* Revelation 18:20.

Twelve times the reference is given to Babylon in the New Testament. In the Old Testament, the Kingdom of Babel was developed into Babylon. Babylon today is Iraq. Does the Babylon in the New Testament have to refer each time to Iraq? Only if the word Babylon is given a literal meaning.

Babylon Given A Non-Literal Meaning

If Babylon is given a non-literal meaning that is as a figure of speech in the Bible then it could be taken as a literary symbol. A figure of speech does convey literal meaning. It is known from tradition that Peter died in Rome as did Paul.

How Is Babylon Used In The Book Of Revelation?

In what sense, is America Babylon? Has Hollywood ever been referred to as Babylon?

Cities could be referred to as Babylon. I cannot understand why any one would interpret Babylon in Revelation as modern Iraq. The standard interpretation of Revelation 17 and 18 is that Babylon here is Rome.

Ecclesiastical Babylon

Revelation 17 refers to the ecclesiastical or religious aspect of Babylon. The woman is a figure of speech for a religious body dressed in ecclesiastical garb, and colors, with religious symbols such as the golden chalice.

In Revelation 18, the commercial aspect of Babylon is the center of the Revelation given to John the Apostle on the Island of Patmos.

Modern Day Nations

Modern day Turkey is found in Revelation chapters 1-4. Israel is found in Revelation chapter 7. China is found in chapters 9 and 16. Jerusalem is referred to in chapters 11 and 14.

America

America is named as the two wings of the eagle in Revelation, chapter 12. The world is referred to as the sea in Revelation, chapter 13. Babylon is referred to in chapters 14, 17, and 18. God and Magog are found in Revelation 20.

America is as much Babylon in the apocalypse of Revelation as is Iraq. Simply because as Babylon is not Iraq, neither is America Iraq. This holds true if the reader understands that such is true if the basis is not a literal interpretation of scripture. If Babylon is interpreted in a symbolic manner understood as a figure of speech then it could stand for a figure of the world. Babylon is Rome in the New Testament book of Revelation.

America Plays A Minor Role

America plays this part in the end time events of the book of the Revelation. America is referred to in Revelation, chapters 6 and 12. Two references are made; one is implied and the other is stated directly.

The writer of the Apocalypse, the Revelation, gives little importance to America in end time events.

America is not a super power during the tribulation period. America will be part of the western power block under the totalitarian rule of the beast and his United States of Europe.

Has America Declined?

One interpretation of America's inability to win the Vietnam war was that of decline.*

*Georgie Anne Geyer, *Guerrilla Prince, The Untold Story of Fidel Castro*, pp. 349-350.

Historically, military defeats or failures to win a war could be interpreted as possibly that nation had declined in power. While this author does not think that this is the proper interpretation of Vietnam as the beginning of the decline of America, such stands in the realm of opinion. Social forces at the time such as the oil embargo in the year 1973 and US decision of not aiding Angola, the Clark Amendment, coupled with the earlier defeat in Vietnam argued for the case of American decline. Castro and the Soviets saw all of this to mean only one thing, that being the decline of America.*

* Ibid, pp. 349-350.

Yet America has well defended herself in the days since the 60's standing for the principle of law and order and human rights throughout the world.

Our next chapter has good news about America's future based on a biblical argument from the Epistle of Romans.

America Under The Antichrist

One of the overlooked and neglected insights of the Greek New Testament afforded us by exegesis is a clear and obvious insight into the origin and identity of the Antichrist. Antichrist is thought to originate as one of the ten horns out of the old Roman Empire.*

*Revelation 13:2, Revelation 17:12.

This is incorrect to interpret the Antichrist, the beast, as one of the ten horns (ten kings) arising out of the Old Roman Empire. A greater hermeneutical error is to interpret Babylon as Iraq. The splendor of the court of Babylon in Revelation, chapter 18 cannot possibly be interpreted as Iraq.

The Antichrist Is A Religious Figure

The Antichrist is a religious cleric who turns into a political leader. Notice that the beast has ten horns and seven heads as found in Revelation 13:1.

"And I saw from the sea a beast rising having ten horns and seven heads and on his ten horns ten diadems, and on his heads a name of Blasphemy."*

*Greek New Testament

The Seven Heads Are Seven Mountains and Seven Kings

In Revelation Chapter 13 and its interpretation, as given in Revelation 17, the seven heads are seven mountains upon which the woman sits, and the seven heads are also seven kings.*

*Revelation 17:9-10.

Rome is the city that has long been known to sit upon seven mountains. The beast, the Antichrist, comes out of the group of seven, seven religious kings, not out of the ten kings who will form the revised Roman empire. The beast, the Antichrist, one of the seven kings, is a religious figure turned political leader. The beast, the Antichrist, replaces ecclesiastical Rome represented by the woman in Revelation 17. Remember that the woman sits on seven mountains and that the woman, a great city, has a kingdom over the peoples and the kings of the earth according to Revelation 17:9-15 and Revelation 17:18.

"And I have heard another voice from heaven saying, start coming out my people from her that you may not share her sins and from her plagues that you may not receive."*

*Greek New Testament.

Parable Of The Tares

In Matthew 13, Jesus taught the parable of the sower and the soils but he also taught the parable of the tares in the same chapter. The parable of the sower and the soils communicates the good sowing of the kingdom of God. The parable of the tares tells us very plainly that alongside the good sowing of the the word of the kingdom, that there will also be a false sowing of the word of the kingdom.

America Now

The Pope visited America in the fall of 1995. It is interesting that this pope is a Polish Pope. I remember as a student at Dallas Theological Seminary those interesting church history classes where I learned of the origin of the Roman Catholic church in 600 A.D., began by Pope Gregory the Great at that time, who was the great administrator of the church.

Political Ideologies And Social Forces

There are many ideologies and forces at work in our country and the world today. Freedom of speech ought not to extend to political leaders who visit this country but come from a country whose political ideology is not in line with the ideology of our land. In my opinion, such leaders should not be allowed entrance into our country. The political ideology of the revolution began in 1917 has spread and lives on today. America is a great country! America works! The American capitalistic system works! The American dream, the goal of many, still works today. The question is whether the people want to work to obtain it. Other countries clearly demonstrate the disastrous effects of the welfare state and socialism's something for nothing. The problem today is that some want something for nothing. They want a paycheck but they are not willing to work for it.

America Works

The material blessings, physical comforts, and the good life are enjoyed by the many, not by the few as in other ideologies and lands. I hope that you are proud to be an American. The American capitalistic system does work in spite of the bad publicity and the propaganda of revolutionary systems.

Who Says That Capitalism Doesn't Work?

Likely in your reading, you have come across negative thought that emphasized that the American system doesn't work. In modern thought today this idea seems to come through that the American capitalistic system does not work any longer.

Socialism Is Not An Alternative

Socialism is the idea of societies emphasizing the state over the individual. Socialism fully developed leads to the revolution and revolutionary thought. The revolution allows only a few individuals to enjoy the wealth, influence, power and comforts that are enjoyed by the many in capitalistic societies.

In America, many ideologies are competing for the allegiance and dedication of the individual. It is in America that determination of the will and hard work of the individual bring about wealth and success. The American dream and the

American capitalistic system still work. The American mind, like the Roman mind of ancient Rome, is very practical.

Lifestyle And Standard Of Living

The lifestyle and standard of living of countless Americans attests to the fact that the American dream works! How many times have you heard it worked for me! That will work!

The Goal of Every American

The goal of every American ought to be first and foremost allegiance to the American Government, the laws of the state and land, and to obey those who are the powers, and law of our day. The Bible clearly teaches that the powers that be are of God.*
*Romans 13:1-7.

Americans Who Believe The Bible

In my opinion and with good reason, Americans who rightly understand the Bible and know Jesus Christ, as their savior by faith, are the most patriotic and obedient to the laws and dictates of our American society. Our loyalty should be to the American flag, and our beloved America. America is the beautiful, the good, and a country that has law, order, and decency.

May we not sacrifice our American spirit and nationalism for a place in the nations. America is still the greatest country on the earth. America has enjoyed richer material blessings and wealth from the hand of Almighty God that any nation has ever enjoyed. It is my opinion, you may agree or disagree, that any ideology, any religion, or religious figure arising in this country or coming to this country should not have our allegiance.

Remember, that the red revolution that began in Russia has spread to many nations. Marxist-Lenin doctrine is obeyed by those who are committed to the continuation of the revolution. This ideology is a threat to our freedom, hope and well being, and welfare of our lives, and future happiness of our families.

Fundamentalism in any religious sphere regardless of the leader that appeals to the minds of Americans to be disloyal to our beloved country and government is to be shunned. Regardless of our religion, culture, social background and social status, our allegiance is to be to the United States of America. The New Testament teaches submission and obedience to the laws of the land.*

*Romans 13:1-7; I Peter 2:13-17

Honor the president! Pay your taxes! Live in civil obedience to the laws of the land. Pray for those who are our leaders!

*I Timothy 2:1-7.

Revolutionary Thought Must Be Stopped

Social revolutionary Lenin-Marxist thought is still alive and spreading. Their propaganda is still being spread and exported throughout our world. If you have studied the Russian Revolution of 1917, then you know that the revolutionaries developed and stressed the importance of propaganda in any struggle for the allegiance of the masses.

Another Danger

The history of the church studied and understood stresses the militancy of religions in the ancient world. Islam and Roman Catholicism have been both militant in church history. Popes raised armies and war followed. Charles Martel stopped the

Moors at the battle of Tours in 732 A.D. The muslims were at the gates of Vienna and if Charles the Hammer had not stopped Islam then, as predetermined by the sovereignty of God, no reformation would have followed. Our loyalty must be to America, not to the Koran, nor to the Church.

There are always those who cry wolf in terms of persecution on the part of born-again Christians. The struggle has always been and always will be between the righteous and those who are not rightly related to God through faith in Jesus Christ.*

*Hebrew Bible, Psalm 37.

Should We Obey God Rather Than Man?

This question arose in the history of the early church whether the apostles and those who followed the apostles' teachings should obey God revealed through Jesus Christ and the Apostles' teachings or man? The Donatists became interesting figures in the history of the early first century church. They obeyed the dictates of the Roman emperor for deification and worship through incense burned to the idol. From A.D. 37 to A.D. 250 when Roman persecutions were universalized rather than localized, the Donatists worshiped the emperor as God and burned the incense to the emperor and his gods. However, after the Roman persecutions ceased at the time of Constantine, and the Edict of Constantine, the Donatists wanted back into the church.

Revolutionary Training Centers

Communism is dead, so they tell us. The cold war is over so they tell us. Yet the revolution has been spread by revolutionary training centers throughout the world. The author was surprised at this very fact having read a book on Fidel Castro.

World Rule

Many ideologies are striving for world rule and dominance. They shall never be satisfied until they rule the world. God has put it in the hearts of men to rule the world. Our allegiance must be not to our background, origins, culture, religious teachings, but to the God ordained powers and government that be. America is a country that has a sense of moral right, law and order and national and international decency. Individual human rights and freedoms contribute to the worth of the individual.

In my opinion, there is a conspiracy abroad that determines right in terms of wealth and progression of their world goals, and political philosophy.

America Wake Up!

The hour is late! The hands of the clock point to 12! May God give us another president like our dearly beloved president Ronald Reagan. We need another president like president Ronald Reagan in the white house. May the American pride and spirit revive in our land! May we by God's grace be able to take pride once again in what it means to be free and to be part of this great land.

America is the land where all races are equal. While not all have the same ability, the same opportunity exists for those who are determined to work. After all, America is not a welfare state. America works!

Jesus Said Watch, That No One Deceive You

Every deception, every religious and political deception is being used in our world today to manipulate the unwary soul. It is interesting that when Jesus was asked about the end of the age in Matthew 24 the deception was the first sign that he gave.

"Watch, that no one deceive you."*

* Matthew 24:4 Greek New Testament.

The American Family Is The Backbone Of This Country.

Those who are informed today understand that the family unit is undergoing stress and change in America.

Loyalty To Family

Faithfulness on the part of husbands and wives to each other will cause the endurance of the family. The Bible teaches one man and one woman forever - only death dissolves the marriage bond. While obviously divorce is an ever increasing present reality, remarriage is not the biblical God ordained pattern. Separation is possible but only the reuniting of the separated married partners is the God ordained marriage bond. Adultery is an unlawful sexual union but it is also a state of barrenness, and no divine blessing forever in this life. The Bible teaches this pattern, one man and one woman forever, as the God ordained pattern for the race. This is not simply the pattern for Christians who have trusted Christ as their personal saviour. God gave marriage to the race, not just to Christians.*

*Romans 7:1-3; I Corinthians 7:10-11; 7:39-40.

No passage of scripture in the Bible teaches divine approval and blessing of a divorced person.

Biblical Roles

The Christian home should practice biblical headship as outlined for us in I Corinthians chapter 11. God the Father is the head of Christ, and Christ is the head of the man. The man is to be in submission to Jesus. The wife is to be in submission and under the authority and command of her loving, understanding, and kind husband. Children are to be in obedience to the parents. Thus order and a chain of authority and command is created within the home.*

* Ephesians 5:22-6:1-4; Colossians 3:18-20; I Peter 3:1-6.

Church Part Of The Kingdom of Heaven

Yet the church that divine parenthesis in the kingdom of heaven has failed for the large part to educate the family as to enduring values and roles. Husbands love your wives! Husbands are to be understanding and kind to your wives. Husbands don't be embittered against your wives. Wives will submit and live in submission and obedience to a loving husband. Children should obey their parents and the Lord for this is pleasing to the Lord.

If You Don't Know Christ As Your Saviour, Trust Him Now

The gospel is that Christ died for our sins, that He was buried and raised, was seen of many witnesses after His resurrection and appeared lastly to Paul.*

*I Corinthians 15:1-11.

You must be born from above to become a child of God. God has no grandchildren! I trust Christ as my personal savior. I understand that Christ died on the cross for me. I see Him hanging there by faith two thousand years, and by faith I trust Christ right now. I am trusting Christ right now and cease to trust anyone or anything else.

"Now as many as have received Him He gave to them power to become children of God to those believing in His name."*

* John 1:12 Greek New Testament.

Only Jesus can save! No religious ceremony or ritual can save you! Only Jesus' blood can save you! I trust Him just now understanding that He died on the cross for me. He took my place!

STUDY QUESTIONS

1. What are the uses of the word Babylon in the New Testament?
2. What aspects does Revelation, chapter 17 refer to?
3. What does Revelation, chapter 18 refer to?
4. What nations are referred to in the Book of Revelation?
5. What chapters refer to America in Revelation?
6. What biblical argument brings us hope about our nation in Romans, chapter 9?
7. How are the ten horns and seven heads of Revelation, chapter 13 to be interpreted?
8. What conclusions can be drawn when we compare Revelation 17:9; 17:15 & 17:18 with Revelation 13?
9. What does the author believe about America?
10. What does Romans 13:1-7 teach?
11. Biblical Christians are more patriotic than others. Why is this true?
12. What are the author's prayers for America?
13. What does John 1:12 teach?

14

AMERICA EXISTS

In order for us to understand the meaning of the words America exists, let's look at the argument that can be built from Romans, chapter 9.

Romans 9:17 is an example of God's sovereign right over Pharaoh. God allowed Pharaoh to exist that the Lord God used Pharaoh to proclaim His divine name and power throughout the earth. Romans 9:18 refers to the divine decree of God. This is based on the Boulema. The Boulema is the divine will or counsel of the Godhead. God is said to be unjust in Romans 9:19 by an imagined objector. Why does He still find fault asks the objector? The reason is that no one is able to resist His will.

As God raised up Pharaoh for His divine purpose, so America exists to proclaim the divine name, Jesus Christ throughout the earth. Yes, America exists to show God's power and proclaim the divine name.*

*Romans 9:17-19

Through the Pharaoh who represented Egypt, God proclaimed Himself throughout the ancient world. While America is a pluralistic society, God is proclaiming his name and demonstrating his power through the Ekklesia. The church is a called out group of men and women from every level of American Society. The body of Christ is people, not buildings.

America Is In Bible Prophecy

America is in bible prophecy by the very fact that America exists. Since God has allowed America to come into being as a new world order since 1776 then one must look for scriptural typology of nations that existed as well. As we ask ourselves for what purpose did this or that nation exist, it was so that God could proclaim His divine name and power throughout the earth through that nation.

God brought Pharaoh into existence for one purpose, to demonstrate His power and proclaim the divine name throughout the earth. Yet Pharaoh and Egypt were not monotheistic, but given to the worship of the gods, a Polytheistic religion. Supernaturally, God proclaimed His name throughout the Earth and His power, at the time of the theological contest between the God of heaven and the gods during the plagues, and the exodus. Each of the plagues recorded in the book of Exodus was against one of the gods of ancient Egypt.

When America Declines?

Have you ever wondered how long America will continue as a superpower? When does America decline as a superpower in the Bible?

A parallel argument that gives an exacting answer to the question can be found in the New Testament book of Romans.

The person of Pharaoh is the divine example used by Paul in Romans, Chapter 9. God allowed Pharaoh to exist, that is, God created Pharaoh or brought him into existence. Pharaoh had arrived at his position of power because of the power and pleasure of the divine will.

Pharaoh Was Used

Through this vessel, the Lord God declared his power and his name throughout the ancient world. The idea of allowing Pharaoh to exist or having created Pharaoh for no other purpose is consistent with the context.*

*Sanday & Headlam, ICC, Romans. Vol., p. 256.

Pharaoh's only justification for his role in history was the divine purpose. While the whole chapter has the subject of God's control over the history of Israel, God's rule is seen in the divine choice of Jacob and the divine rejection of Esau. The hebraism to love means to choose and to hate is to reject. Jacob, I have chosen, but Esau, I have rejected.

God's Control Over Israel

God's rule is due to His divine will. The choice of the divine will is traced to the mercy of God and God's compassion. Pharaoh, of Egypt, is interjected in Paul's divine argument in Romans 9:18 as an example of divine hardening.

"So then whom He wills He shows mercy, whom He wills He hardens."*

* Greek New Testament, Romans, 9:18.

Pharaoh's only justification for existence was the divine purpose. If this is true, and the Bible teaches that it is, then just how sovereign is God?

God's Will

The divine purpose, the divine will, was to proclaim the divine name and power throughout the earth. This occurred at the time of the plagues in the book of Exodus, and the Exodus from Egypt in 1445 B.C.

God's Will Completed

With the plagues finished, and Israel's Exodus, Pharaoh had served the divine purpose.

America Exists, So What?

Based on the parallel between Egypt and America, we assert with confidence that America exists. America exists only for the divine purpose. God has used America to proclaim the divine name Jesus Christ, and His power throughout America and the rest of the earth.

When America Ceases

America will decline when America ceases to serve the divine purpose any longer. The history of America has been one of advancing the missionary cause and the Christian faith.

America will decline when America ceases to be needed in the divine purpose. This will occur at the Rapture of the church. America's real church raptured - the redeemed of her ages - America will decline.*

* 2 Thess. 2:3-12

The mystery of lawlessness will be released with a flood of lawlessness and crime. Crime is a great problem in America's cities at the present time. The mystery of lawlessness will come to completion when the Antichrist is revealed at that time in Rome.

STUDY QUESTIONS

1. How is the author's argument for America exists" based on Romans chapter 9:17 & 18?
2. Based on Romans 9:17-19, why does America exist?
3. How can this be true in a pluralistic society?
4. Why did God allow Pharaoh to exist?
5. How sovereign is God?
6. What is the Hebraism is Romans 9 concerning Jacob and Esau?
7. What is the significance of the divine will in Romans, chapter 9?
8. Has God foreordained the events and the means to accomplish the event?
9. When will America decline?

15

GOD AND AMERICA

America's Future

America's future has been predetermined by the sovereign God. A better question than, "Is America in Prophecy," is, "How far does God's sovereignty extend?"

The future of America is fixed both in terms of her allotted time as a nation and also her boundaries. The divine decree purpose of God in eternity past included the nations as well.

America No Mention in Daniel

In Daniel, chapters 2 and 7, the world empires decreed by God in eternity past, are revealed to the prophet. Babylon, Medio-Persia, Greece, Rome, the yet future revived Roman empire, and Messiah's kingdom. No mention is made in these chapters of the prophecies concerning the gentile world empire, America.

God's Wonderful Plan For Our Lives

God's purpose was formed based on the counsel of his own will. God is not influenced by anyone outside of himself. He adopted the plan of the universe based on His own good pleasure for His glory.*
  *Eph. 1:1-14

Things Which Must Come To Pass

The decree of God is efficacious in that what he decreed is certain. What the Lord God has foreordained must come to pass. God by His own omnipotence is permitting these events to occur through the agency of his own creatures.*
  * Isaiah 14:27; 43:13; 45:1.
  The Gentile will obey God's divine decree and do all His will.

America's Objections Answered

The infinite wisdom and omniscience of God is behind the eternal decree of God. The fact of God's unlimited knowledge of all things actual and possible behind the plan differentiates it from fatalism. In a fatalistic, pagan view of life, all things are working on the basis of the trinity of luck, time, chance or randomness, and fate. God's infinite mind planned all things, whatsoever comes to pass in eternity past. God's sovereign will make it past reality with the continuing results being worked out in history.

God's Plan Included Not Only The End, But The Means.

Yes, God foreordained all that comes to pass, but also the means to accomplish that end. Inclusion of the means as well as the end moves the child of God from the grandstand on to the stage with God. God has decreed to employ human beings to bring the divine decree to fulfillment.

The Decree of God Is Incompatible With Man's Free Will

The decree stresses the fact of man's responsibility and will. Such is included in the plan because God is completely in control. (Sovereign) There is no such thing as an absolutely free will, not even in God. (Romans 9:15)
    * Eph. 1:11; Job 36:22-23; Isaiah 40:13-14; Rom. 11:34; I Cor. 2:16; Psalm 115:3; Psalm 136:26; Daniel 4:35; Romans 11:36; Matthew 11:26; Roman 8:29-30; 9:15-18; Eph. 1:5.
    * Charles Hodge, Systematic Theology, Vol. I, p. 441.
    There is nothing man can do to make God merciful.*
    *Romans 9:16.
    The sovereignty of God is seen in His allowing Pharaoh to exist to show his power and to proclaim His name.*
    *Romans 9:17.
    God is free to show mercy to whom He wills or as with Pharaoh to harden whom He wills based on the decision made within the divine decree in eternity past.*
    *Romans 9:18.

The Objector Might Say

Why does He yet find fault? The reason given in the test is that who can resist His will? The apostle affirms the divine sovereignty of God over his creatures in Romans 9:20 and 9:21. His right to predestine beforehand one vessel to wrath and another to mercy is seen as part of His divine sovereignty.
* Romans 9:22-23.

Do Read Romans 9:22-23

The Bible teaches double destiny theory as set forth in this passage. The basis of destiny is God's choice as seen in Romans 9:24. Those destined are those whom He chose in eternity past before the world began.

America Is Predestinated

Predestination is defined as the destiny of the elect. (Ephesians 1:5) Predestination is not pretribution meaning to pass by the non-elect because of their lost estate in Adam. This is sufficient to damn the non-elect, but the Bible does not teach pretribution in relationship to the non-elect.

The Decree of God Distorts God's Justice

The deliberate purpose or decree of God is said to be a distortion of justice. The question of Romans 9:19 is not allowed in God's court room. As the potter has the right over the clay, so God as the creator has the right over man.*
*Romans 9:20-21.

God has the right over America to do as He planned in eternity past.

Man Is Not Able To Do Anything

Paul raises the question in Romans 9:22-4 that man is not able to do anything if this was God's eternal purpose. These are first class conditions in the greek language that assume the reality of the fact. God has destined from eternity past vessels fitted beforehand for destruction. Vessels of wrath were fitted for destruction. God's sovereignty is to be seen in Romans 9:22. God determined beforehand what comes to pass. The willing of Romans 9:22 has a two-fold reference. First, to show His wrath and to make His power known; second, to make known the riches of His glory upon vessels of mercy.*

*Romans 9:22-23.

Thus God has fitted vessels of wrath to destruction in order that He may make known the wealth of His glory upon vessels of mercy prepared beforehand for glory.*

*Charles Hodge, Systematic Theology, Vol I-III.

*Mathers, Lectures, Faith Theological Seminary, Elkins Park, PA, Theology I, 1989-1990.

The basis of God's predestination purposes is His election
God is not unrighteous in His choice of Jacob over Esau*
*Romans 9:14.

His election is traced to His divine sovereignty. Predestination means destiny determined before the foundation of the world. Ephesians 1 teaches the destination of the elect by election and predestination before the foundation of the world. Eternity past is before the created world and time began.*

*Liddel & Scott, Greek English Lexicon, p 1493.

The following tests of the new testament teach the truth of our destiny determined beforehand.* The Greek verb *proorizo* means to divide or separate from as a boundary or a border, mark out, ordain, determine, mark-out boundaries by stones.

The nuance in our case is to ordain or determine, to mark out or set apart beforehand.

*Acts 4:28; Romans 8:29-30; I Cor. 27; Ephesians 1:5; Ephesians 1:11.

Luther's *Bondage Of The Will* points out that free will is used only of God in the Psalms. Free will is never used of man in the Bible. Those who refer to 'whosever will" in Romans should understand that Paul quotes Joel where the "whosoever will" are saints during the tribulation elected to salvation in eternity past.

The Decree Of God Makes God The Author Of Sin

God permitted the presence of sin in his plan. Why God permitted sin we do not know. We believe by faith, the Word of God's revelation, that God chose the best plan to bring the most glory to Himself. God hates sin.*

*Psalm 5:5.

Yet man is given the responsibility for his sin.

God Moves On Men

God moves on man who thinks that he is acting independently, yet he is fulfilling the divine decreed will.

The Decree of God Kills Missionary Zeal

As a surface argument, it appears to be valid. If we think for a moment of Paul, the apostle, his life, ministry and writings give us more information on the sovereignty and decree of God

than anyone else. Yet Paul was the greatest missionary who ever lived. History becomes the unfolding of the eternal purposes of God.*
   *Acts 2:23; 4:27-28.

I'm Not A Child of Wrath

God's sovereign right to save or damn is the point of the biblical concept of predestination taught by the God breathed book of the Bible.

Preterition Is Not Defined As Passing By The Non-elect

The passing by of the non-elect is not a biblical teaching. Predestination is not preterition meaning to pass by the non-elect because of their lost estate in Adam. This is sufficient to damn the non-elect but the Bible does not teach this in regard to them. The ninth chapter of Romans argues in favor of the double predestination theory as actual fact in eternity past. God did not have to save anyone but He elected to in eternity past. Paul raises the question that is unanswerable because as the sovereign potter, God has the right to do so that he might show His kindness to vessels of mercy fitted for glory.*
   * Romans 9:22-23.

What Does All This Mean For America?

America, both the nation and its people, are sovereignly predetermined both as to their span of rule, boundaries, and destination. God chose man's destiny rather than the misguided concept in our thinking that men decide their destiny.

Resting In God's Character

We can rest in the knowledge of the infinite perfection of the character of God.

The Lord God's infinity means that He fills heaven and earth. God is exalted above all that man thinks or knows, and is without end in terms of His being and perfections. It is not possible to assign a limitation to the essence of God.

God Near and Far Off At The Same Time

He fills the heavens and the earth with His whole person. Jeremiah 23:23 & 24 tell us of the greatness of the infinity of God. He is not diffused nor divided in His person and presence. The Psalmist, in Psalm 139, tells the truth of God's presence with His whole being whether heaven, the earth or the sea. Heaven and the heaven of heavens cannot contain God.*

* I Kings 8:27.

God is omnipresent in all the heavens yet separate from and greater than the heavens.*

*Charles Hodge, Systematic Theology, Vol. I Part 1, pp. 381-382.

The greatness of God is unsearchable. Men are instructed to respond to the infinity of God by praising Him. God is free from all limitations. God is without end.*

*Psalm 145:3.

STUDY QUESTIONS

1. What is the better question than "Is America in prophecy?"
2. Is America mentioned in Daniel 2 & 7?
3. What was God's purpose (The Divine Decree) based on?
4. What was the basis for the decree?
5. What does Isaiah 14:27, 43:13 and 45:1 teach?
6. Why is the eternal decree of God not fatalism?
7. How far does God's divine sovereignty extend? (See Romans 9:22-23)
8. Predestination is the destiny of the elect. T or F
9. God did not pass over the non-elect in Adam. Why is this a true statement?
10. What question is not allowed in God's courtroom? (See Romans 9:19-20)
11. Romans 9:22-24 are first class conditions that assume the reality of the fact -- what did God do?
12. The basis of God's predestination is His election. What is His election traced to. (Romans 9:14-15)
13. The ninth chapter of Romans argues in favor of the double predestination theory. T or F
14. What does all this mean for America?

16

AMERICA'S GRAVE DANGER

Believing The Lie!

During the tribulation period, America will face the grave danger of being faced with the choice of believing the lie. At the revelation of the totalitarian dictator, the lie will be universally circulated. The Antichrist is God.

The acceptance of the name or number of Antichrist will bring disastrous consequences both on an individual and national level.

God Sends The Work Of Error

The Lord God will send them the work of error. The Antichrist's coming will be based on the supernatural workings of Satan with all power, signs, and false wonders. This is further described as with all deceit of unrighteousness. Why will there be such deception on America during the tribulation? The answer is a simple one. At that time, Americans have not received the love of the truth that saves them. Instead, they have taken pleasure in unrighteousness rather than having believed the truth.*

* 2 Thess: 2:7-12; Revelation: 13:8; 17:8.

Who Will Believe The Lie?

Those whose names have not been written down from before the foundation of the world will believe the lie.*

* Revelation: 13:8;11

In 1917, The Bolshevik revolution toppled the Czar's regime of Russia. The leadership and those associated with it, vowed they would never turn off that road. Russian propaganda has America believing that communism has died. Russia is in disarray. The USSR is no more. The Bible knew nothing of a USSR, but the Bible speaks of the military totalitarian giant, the King of the North, modern day Russia.*

*J.M. Thompson *Revolutionary Russia, 1917*

Is It Possible?

All too few people realize the place of propaganda in the plan of those committed to the revolution and it's triumph. Could Russian propaganda deceive America into thinking that they were a democratic free society? Could Russia use her people to think that they are controlling and directing Russia?

It may well be that recent Russian leaders were and are soft. Don't be surprised if a Russian leader comes to the forefront shortly, who is a hard line totalitarian revolutionist!

The Genius Of The Russian Empire

They may have wanted to end the use of the word communists since, from an American perspective, it is a nasty word. It conveys all sorts of emotional overtones. Communist conveys from the idea of all things in common. No, the Bible in Acts 2 does not teach communism. The early Jewish Christians had all things in common because of the persecutions that arose against the early church.

The Revolution Continues

While all report that communism has died, the revolution spread by red revolutionary Guerrillas continues throughout the earth. The author reading G.A. Geyer's *"Guerrilla Prince"* was astounded at the extent of the Guerrilla network and Castro's contribution to the revolution. Just recently, Guerrillas in Mexico have staged rebellions similar to those once staged in Cuba. Trotsky had the idea of the continuing of the revolution.

Mistake! Mistake!

America must not disarm itself because Russia has great military might even today. A hidden Russian goal of world rule is what the Bible portrays of Russia in the end times.

Ultimately, the revolution prepares the world for the Antichrist.

The revelation of the antichrist in the end times will demonstrate the triumph of communism. Since the Antichrist, like communism, will be the worship of man rather than God.

It Could Be Fatal

One of the mistakes that America may well be making is thinking that Russia is no longer a threat to our society. After all, is not the current thinking, the cold war is over?

Totalitarian Ideology

It is a hard reality to face the fact of the totalitarian mentality. Worse still is the hard reality that the totalitarian reality is much alive in our world.

The Bible tells us that the world dictator worships the god of military might.*

* Daniel 11:36-38

Yes, the Bible teaches the great military strength of Russia in end time events. The Russians are able to put three complete armies in the field during the Armageddon campaign.

How Lenin And The Bolsheviks Came To Power

The needs of the masses in Russia, in 1917, were not being met. This drove the peasant population, the workers, and soldiers to become increasingly radicalized. The Russian dream was no longer possible for the masses! According to J. M. Thompson in his book *"Revolutionary Russia, 1917"*, The five issues that brought Lenin and his Bolshevik party to power were peace, land, bread, worker's control, and fears of counter-revolution.

The revolution in Russia in 1917 gave fulfillment to the needs and material dreams of the Russian populace.*

* J.M. Thompson, *Revolutionary Russia, 1917*, pp. 125-35. IBID p 165.

Lenin And His Bolsheviks

They provided extensive propaganda which was published in papers and journals. The various revolutionary groups had their hopes fulfilled. The dissemination of the ideas of the Bolshevik party was spread to the masses. The Russian masses knew what they were thinking.

Lenin knew that World War I had weakened world capitalism. This made a revolution possible for Lenin and his Bolsheviks. Lenin believed that the workers would come to power because of the prevailing conditions in Russia at that time. The proletariat was stronger than the Bourgeoisie. The land hunger of the peasants and general discontent that the war produced, created a revolutionary spirit in Russia. Coupled to all of this was Trotsky's theory of permanent revolution. Yes, unfortunately, the revolution that began in Russia in 1917 has spread to much of our world.*

*Robert V. Daniels, *Red October*, pp. 16-35

What Time Is It?

It is the Times of the Gentiles with God. This day of Gentile world rule, by the nations descended from Noah, began with the fall of Jerusalem in 586 BC. Judah and Jerusalem fell to Nebuchadnezzar and the Babylonians. (Modern day Iraq).

The Times of the Gentiles continues until Christ's Second Coming but do not have to be fulfilled. This aorist passive subjunctive is the mood of probability and is the farthest removed from reality. After all, the nations have had 2000 years and they can't get it together.

The Second Coming of Christ will bring about the introduction of the dispensation of the kingdom on the earth. Christ's 1000 year rule will be from Mount Zion.

The day of grace, the dispensation of grace that began on the day of Pentecos, and will close with the Rapture, is the day of the fullness of the gentiles. Soon the day of Christ will end!

Opportunity is still available for you to trust Christ as your savior. Begin to trust Christ now, to bring you into a right relationship with God.

Beyond Our Time has developed fully the question of America in prophecy. The role and destiny of America has been shown within the framework of established Bible prophecies.

STUDY QUESTIONS

1. What grave danger does America face during the tribulation period?
2. What is the lie?
3. What is the work of error? (2 Thess. 2:7-12)
4. Who will believe the lie?
5. What king does Bible prophecy speak of Russia as?
6. What is the meaning of the biblical phrase "The Times of the Gentiles?"
7. Christ's Second Coming, not the Rapture which occurred seven years earlier, will herald in what dispensation?